WEYMOUTH

Through Old Photographs

YVETTE STAELENS

DORSET BOOKS

First published in Great Britain in 1989 by Dorset Books

Copyright text © Yvette Staelens 1989

Illustrations © Weymouth Museum

British Library Cataloguing-in-Publication Data

Staelens, Yvette J. E.
    Weymouth through old photographs.
    1. Dorset. Weymouth, history
    I. Title
    942.3'35

    ISBN 1–871164–05–2

Printed and bound in Great Britain by BPCC Wheatons Ltd

DORSET BOOKS

An imprint of Wheaton Publishers Ltd. A member of Maxwell/Pergamon Publishing Corporation plc

Wheaton Publishers Ltd
Hennock Road, Marsh Barton, Exeter, Devon EX2 8RP
Tel: 0392 74121; Telex 42794 (WHEATN G)

SALES
Direct sales enquires to Dorset Books at the address above.

ACKNOWLEDGEMENTS

The photographs in this book are from the Weymouth Museum Archive and copyright is retained by the museum.

The author is indebted to the staff for their comments and assistance, and also to Nigel Pope.

For Mr and Mrs S.

CONTENTS

INTRODUCTION

Millions of photographs have been taken in Weymouth over the years, ending up in albums worldwide. Most will never find their way into public collections but will retain nostalgic value, only to their owners. Happily some good collections of local photographs have been gathered in Dorset and it is examples from the Weymouth Museum archive that are presented here.

Weymouth today comprises the twin towns of Weymouth and Melcombe Regis, joined officially by Royal Charter in 1571. The old town of Weymouth lies on the far side of the harbour, away from the beach, and still gives the impression of a settlement that has evolved randomly according to local need. No town planning here; the streets have developed around natural features, winding and undulating up the hill and down along the quayside.

When the town turned its back on the harbour to concentrate on the beach, Melcombe Regis saw rapid development whilst Weymouth slowly declined. This division is dramatically reflected in the photographic legacy, for looking through the public collections, it is evident that Melcombe photographs predominate. It seems that there was little on the Weymouth side to attract the photographer, amateur or professional, therefore it is somewhat perplexing to admit that no specific Weymouth photographs are included in this selection; however this statement is not intended as an apology, but rather as a plea.

All too often, old photographs are first to go when the possessions of the recently deceased are sorted through. Old letters, faded snapshots and press cuttings tend to be discarded, destined for the town dump or garden bonfire. How very sad this seems, when such fragments could easily be packed together and presented to a local library or museum as a collection of family papers. Thankfully, many such collections have been presented by forward-thinking individuals and some excellent material can be found particularly in the borough archives. Much has not been saved and some only through the most fortuitous circumstances, of these, a classic story is that of the 'Sherren Papers'.

In 1840, the Town Council's archive committee decided to sort out the papers contained in a very heavy chest in their possession. Some documents were kept, others discarded and it is the 'discarded' items that are now known as the 'Sherren Papers'. The story is that as they were being taken out to be used as kindling for fires, a Mr Barlow had the idea of contacting James Sherren (who was publishing a Weymouth Guide at the time), thinking he might find them useful. Sherren retrieved the papers in the 'most wretched condition imaginable — saturated with damp and mildew and almost torn to shreds.' He carefully dried and restored them, devoted several months of his time to mounting fragile items and then catalogued them in numbered portfolios. Mr Sherren instantly recognised their 'very rare and singular value' and made them available to whoever wished to view them. A commendable feat of public-spiritedness. Some years later however, he was the recipient of anonymous letters and scandalous allegations that he had procured the documents by dubious means. In addition, once the 'value' of the papers was realised, there were initiatives from the council to retrieve them also. Mr Sherren was justifiably astonished, and he published a full statement regarding the recent history of the papers and his role in saving them from destruction. Also, he stated that it was his intention to care for them on behalf of the people of Weymouth since he was 'not quite sure but that the next generation may send men to the council chamber similar to those of the past generation – no lovers of the rare and valuable – and again consign them to the waste paper basket.' His legacy remains today as the most remarkable collection of local history papers in the borough.

In our disposable society, thousands of unique documents, ephemera and photographs are discarded daily. In Weymouth, irreplaceable photographs of the town and its people are disappearing and many of those remaining are unidentified. Mystery photographs are tantalising, perhaps pretty to look at but historically valueless. Strangers stare out from beach huts, bath chairs and the corner shop, locations are uncertain – photographs which should be fascinating historical evidence, remain enigmatic. However, it is here that you can help. Next time you delve in that suitcase for an elusive family snapshot, why not haul the whole lot out, gather the family, and have fun identifying 'Uncle Cyril on Preston Beach in 1925', or your grandmother's wedding at Holy Trinity Church in 1912, and then pencil the details on the back?

The photographs presented here are a tiny selection of a vast communal inheritance. From them we can learn a little about how people looked and lived in the recent past in our town. The art of full enjoyment of these images however lies in understanding that they capture only a moment and it is useful to try to imagine what was happening both before and after 'the moment'. Remember also that these pictures give a misleading monochrome impression of the past. They lack colour, sound and smell. By attempting to imagine these sensations in relation to the photographs presented here, it is possible to give these fleeting shadows life; they can then become windows through which we may glimpse incidents in the daily life of this lovely seaside town.

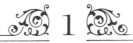

1

The Port and Harbour

Rights to the harbour have long been disputed between the twin ports of Weymouth and Melcombe Regis. The shared harbour was the heart of these maritime settlements, therefore, rights and privileges were jealously guarded.

Mention of the ports is first made around 1100 when they were granted to the prior and convent of St Swithun of Winchester. In 1254 Melcombe Regis passed to Eleanor of Castille as a wedding gift and her coat of arms can still be seen today in the arms of the borough, flying from the rear mast of the ship.

The peaceful scene here, belies the fascinating and often violent past of Weymouth's maritime community. Throughout history the trade of merchant has merged with pirate, smuggler and privateer since little distinction was made between goods acquired through trade or raid. Weymouth men were tough, uncompromising seafarers and no opportunity was ever wasted.

An incident recorded in the borough archives for 1322 is typical of their activities. It involves a certain William de Ekkeworth, a Tavistock man in possession of a ship laden with cloth, linen, iron, wax and other sundry cargo. He complained that he had been attacked and boarded by certain persons of 'Waymeue' and Portland who had carried away the merchandise and scuttled the ship. It is not known whether the culprits were ever caught.

In later days privateering was equally lucrative and it is interesting to note that more letters of marque were issued to Weymouth shipping during the seventeenth and eighteenth centuries than to any other south coast port. Letters of marque were obtained from the Lord High Admiral and entitled the bearers to take foreign ships as 'prizes'. This was official piracy and Weymouth men grasped the opportunity eagerly.

The days of piracy were fortunately long over for Weymouth when this photograph was taken in 1898.

The George Inn, Custom House Quay. All is calm as the photographer glides across the harbour for this late nineteenth-century photograph. The inn is probably named after Weymouth's most famous tourist, King George III, who enjoyed many pleasant stays in the resort from 1789 until 1805.

Retired watermen pose for a Victorian photographer outside Devonshire Buildings on the Esplanade. They are Peter Green, B. Beall (nicknamed 'Nisey'), Tom Vye, J. Bolt and T. Talbot. Ex-mariners such as these tended to live around the harbour and do odd jobs in order to keep them out of the workhouse. Peter Green was quite a celebrity in his day — it was said that when he was a baby, he had been kissed by King George III. He had also served on H.M.S. *Victory* at Trafalgar.

Sail power has brought many things to Weymouth including prehistoric settlers, Roman goods, and in the medieval period, the bubonic plague.

In the thirteenth century the port assumed great importance, particularly through the export of wool and the import of wine. Later there was extensive trade with Spain, France, Portugal and Venice.

These vessels were amongst the last tall ships to ply into Weymouth with their cargoes of Baltic timber. This picture dates from the late nineteenth century.

Celebrations, processions and presentations have always been enthusiastically supported in the town and here a large crowd witnesses the unveiling of the Clark-Endicott Memorial, on 2 June 1914. The memorial commemorates New World emigrants who sailed from Weymouth led by Richard Clark and John Endicott. Endicott left Weymouth in June 1628 in the *Abigail* and was destined to become the first governor of Massachusetts.

The unveiling was performed by the stylish American lady standing at the table. Mrs Joseph Chamberlain was a direct descendant of John Endicott.

Weymouth's Town Bridge has been rebuilt over several centuries in timber, stone and steel. This view from 1880 shows workmen on the temporary wooden draw-bridge used during the reconstruction of the Town Bridge. It links St Nicholas Street to Old Chapelhay Steps.

This postcard of a convict ship still sold well in Weymouth long after the ship had left port. The vessel had been a popular tourist attraction at the turn of the century, and many came to peer into her gloomy hold to view the squalid conditions endured by the prisoners. The ship had transported convicts to Australia and at the end of her working life, she was purchased by an entrepreneur who toured her around the south coast.

Two convict ships, the *Betty* and the *Happy Return* sailed from Weymouth after the failed Monmouth Rebellion of 1685. A year later, they landed in Barbados.

On 4 July 1930, the new Town Bridge was opened by H.R.H. The Duke of York. The first bridge linking Weymouth and Melcombe Regis was built in the late sixteenth century and since then six successive bridges have spanned the harbour. First under the new bridge were excited Weymouth schoolchildren aboard Cosens' paddle steamer *Empress*.

Horse-drawn carts wait outside Sanders' depot on the quayside, in about 1895. Sanders' were major wholesalers in the town, importing coal from as far away as the ports on the Tyne.

The building was originally designed as a fish market and opened in time for Christmas 1855.

The fish market was subsequently transferred to a new Market Hall in St Mary's Street and the building was used as a storage depot.

Today the building is undergoing restoration and has resumed its original function as a fish market.

It is easy to forget that Weymouth once imported vast quantities of fresh produce from the Channel Islands. This 1930s photograph shows broccoli being unloaded by Weymouth dockers.

The crew of the Weymouth lifeboat *Friern Watch* in 1912. **Back row:** Sam Edwards, C. Vallance, Joe Doucher (2nd coxswain), J. Spranklin snr (coxswain), Mark Frowde (Honorary Secretary), J. Moggridge, Joe Vine, Coastguard Freeman, A. Mabb, B. Hodder (shore signalman). **Front row:** J. S. Spranklin, Bob Cook, Herb Brown (bowman), R. Marks, Sam Beale, Jock Gillingham, Coastguard Moloney, Albert Burt.

    Friern Watch was a 38-foot Watson class twelve-oared sailing lifeboat. She was launched twenty-four times and saved nineteen lives.

Weymouth as a resort has always been famous for paddle steamer trips with the local firm of Cosens running excursions as far as Dartmouth in the west and the Isle of Wight in the east. This is the *Albert Victor* seen alongside one of the clinker-built rowing boats available for hire from the harbour.

The *Albert Victor* was built at South Shields in 1883 and purchased by Cosens in 1889. She saw service as a pleasure steamer, tug and as a temporary 'liberty boat' for the Royal Naval Squadron at anchor in Weymouth Bay.

The crew of the *Victoria* paddle steamer. Built in 1884 the *Victoria* was considered to be the most graceful of all paddle steamers. She was a Weymouth regular and one of the best remembered. In this photograph of around 1900, the crew wear smart reefer jackets with shiny brass buttons topped with navy style caps. Note also the fishermen's jerseys and the reclining gentleman who appears to be wearing a knitted beret. Hand-knitted sweaters provided both warmth and comfort but were also useful for identification when maritime fatalities occurred. Many villages and even individual families had their own distinctive patterns knitted into their sweaters.

Monarch was built in 1888 and was the biggest excursion boat on the south coast. In her early days she made regular cross-Channel trips to Cherbourg and the Channel Islands. However, most of her working life involved sailing between Bournemouth and Swanage.

Sail and steam in Weymouth Harbour *c.* 1900. The paddle steamer *Brodick Castle* lies at her mooring adjacent to a fine three-masted sailing ship.

The crew of *Brodick Castle* in a photograph of 1903. Amidst the smart uniforms of the cabin crew, the stokers can be easily identified by their flat caps and the rough scarves tied around their necks.

There has been a quayside tramway at Weymouth Harbour since 1865. In 1880 the original horse-drawn waggons were replaced with steam traction engines and nine years later the route was used to link up with the GWR ferry service to the Channel Islands. This service was initially operated by the screw steamers *Gazelle* and *Lynx* and embarkation was from a newly constructed passenger landing stage and baggage hall located on the pier.

Relations between the port and the Channel Islands were however, not always so amicable. In the seventeenth century, Weymouth citizens complained bitterly that Jerseymen were responsible for much local piracy and plundering. In fact, the situation grew so bad, that the Corporation was forced to send Colonel John Heane, commander of the Weymouth and Sandsfoot garrison, 'to reduce that island'.

A Channel Islands service was initially operated by small sailing cutters of about 80 tons, and depending on the weather, the voyage took between 18 hours and 2 weeks. Steamers made their first appearance around 1820, but they were unreliable and always breaking down. It was not until 1889 when screw steamers took over that a regular service became possible. This photograph shows the P.S. *St Julien*, boarding in August 1929.

During the war years, along with many sister ships, she did valuable service as a transport and hospital ship. She was at Anzio, Italy, in 1943 and later took part in the Normandy landings of 1944.

In 1945, she resumed her cross-Channel duties, continuing in service until September 1960 when she was towed to Antwerp for breaking. Her ship's bell has been preserved and is now in Weymouth Museum.

The king arrives to review the Fleet in Weymouth Bay. The pier has hosted many royal visitors and here King George V is greeted by 3000 cheering schoolchildren for his naval review of 1912.

In July 1933, Edward, Prince of Wales, arrived to open the reconstructed harbour works and to confirm the recent extension to the borough boundaries. Here, sea scouts greet him on the pier. Spot the troupe leader with his 'Box Brownie' camera, acquiring a snapshot momento of the occasion.

In July 1939, the town turned out to greet the king and queen accompanied by the princesses Elizabeth and Margaret Rose. The royal family had travelled by train to Weymouth in order to embark on the royal yacht *Victoria and Albert*. Here, Town Clerk, Percy Smallman watches closely as bouquets are presented to the princesses.

2

The Beach

Weymouth's pride has always been its fine sandy beach and beautiful bay; features that have attracted visitors in their thousands to sample the pleasures of a traditional seaside holiday.

In the eighteenth century, the habit of 'taking the waters' at the spa towns, and of sea bathing at coastal resorts, became extremely popular in fashionable society. The idea of sea bathing became quite a craze however, after King George III gave it the royal seal of approval by stepping out of a bathing machine on Weymouth Sands in 1789.

This was his first visit to Weymouth, and for many years afterwards, he and his family enjoyed regular summer vacations here. Royal patronage brought the rich who required good lodgings and entertainment. Weymouth's future as a resort was established. The twin towns that had once fought over harbour rights, now focused upon assets hitherto unrecognised; the superb bay, picturesque coastline and healthy climate.

By the 1930s, when this photograph was taken, the traditional seaside holiday had become a part of the English lifestyle. The small boy clutching his toy yacht in the centre of this picture is however a charming reminder of the town's origins: the age of sail, when the bay witnessed the sinister activities of smugglers, the tearful farewells of New World colonists, and in 1588, the terrible sight of a thin dark line of sail on the horizon – the mighty Spanish Armada.

A view of around 1870.

Another early photograph of the southern end of the Esplanade showing a quiet deserted scene. The Nothe Fort can be clearly seen on the headland at the harbour entrance.

This promontory has always been of great strategic importance and is the site of early fortifications. The foundations of the present Nothe Fort were laid in 1860, with work being completed by both Royal Engineers and Portland Prison inmates. The fort's military use ceased at the end of the Second World War and it has recently been refurbished by Weymouth Civic Society. It is open to the public in the summer months.

The strict moral codes of the Victorian period demanded that only young children should paddle and play bare-legged on the beach. Men and women remained completely clothed on the sands.

Sea bathing originally required discrete changing facilities and to accommodate this need, the bathing machine was invented in the eighteenth century. This is the royal bathing machine of King George III, first used by His Majesty in 1789. It remained in use on the beach until the demise of individual machines at the beginning of the twentieth century. These were replaced by larger communal bathing saloons, beach huts and private tents.

Today, the royal bathing machine has been carefully restored and is a key exhibit at Weymouth Museum.

THE ESPLANADE.

The Esplanade at the turn of the century. The bath chairs (seen on the left) and the bathing machines (to the right), were available for hire to those that could afford them. Sea bathing was seen as both fashionable and therapeutic and in the 1880s there were around sixty bathing machines operating from Weymouth Sands.

Mr H.J. Hill was Weymouth's last licensed bath chair man. Bath chairs were another eighteenth-century invention, having been devised by James Heath of Bath around 1750. For the next three-quarters of a century they were to rival the sedan chair and ultimately supersede it, becoming especially popular in Victorian seaside resorts.

Mr Hill's passenger in this 1930s photograph is Rev. Hawkins of Greenhill.

An 1890s view of the northern end of the Esplanade. The large building projecting from the terrace is the Hotel Burdon (now Prince Regent), once the resort's premier hotel. The Burdon and adjacent terrace, were completed in Georgian style in 1855.

From here, guests might amble across the road to enjoy the sea air and perhaps hire one of the sailing boats seen here drawn up on the beach.

A fine view of the beach taken at the turn of the century. The 'Geisha Boys' show is attracting a large audience, whilst the fashionable and inquisitive promenade along the Esplanade to see and be seen.

Greenhill Gardens were laid out in formal style in 1872, and counterbalanced the Alexandra Gardens at the opposite end of the Esplanade. They provided a lovely location for an afternoon stroll and were famous for their floral clock.

Whilst the evening illuminations added yet more appeal to a very attractive twentieth-century facility, the view was far from delightful in the seventeenth century. At this time the gallows were sited at Greenhill and amongst various executions here, by far the most gruesome must have been those of the men condemned by the infamous Judge Jeffreys in 1685, to be hung, drawn and quartered. Twelve men died on the scaffold and their dismembered bodies were then displayed around the town and surrounding villages.

THE FLORAL CLOCK, WEYMOUTH

A crowded beach scene of the 1920s. Note that the large bathing saloons have replaced all of the old horse-drawn bathing machines. Also notice the increase in beach attractions.

As well as the traditional pastimes of fishing, playing in the sand, boat trips and donkey rides, fun could be had watching firework displays, vaudeville shows and Punch and Judy.

Sand modelling contest, 1903. Sponsored by Bovril, this competition has attracted a large crowd.

Weymouth sand is ideal for sand modelling and today the resort boasts arguably the finest sand modeller in the country, Fred Darrington. His wonderfully detailed and often topical models can be enjoyed on the beach each summer.

Sadly, the names of the these expert sand modellers have not been recorded.

Goat carriages could be hired for children's rides on the sands from the early 1900s. Goats were harnessed in pairs to specially-constructed ornate carts like this example, made of wickerwork with padded leather upholstery. It is surprising to note however, that goats were allowed to keep their vicious-looking horns.

Weymouth donkeys. An essential part of a child's seaside holiday.

Beach attractions were many and varied, but none more so than this surprise visitor which arrived on Christmas Day in 1930. This is the French ketch *L'Arguenon*, which had been blown on to the beach in a storm. She remained stranded here for several days and was much photographed. Happily she was in good condition and was eventually towed off.

Visits of the Home Fleet were a popular sight in the bay until 1914, when Portland ceased to be a base for the Channel Fleet. The Weymouth paddle steamers would chug out to the ships, and sailors would enjoy their shore leave sampling the resort's attractions — even if that meant a doze on the beach.

However, not everyone was pleased with the regular invasions of mariners. For example, the mayor in 1865, Mr J. Ayling, was 'most concerned to protect Weymouth society, particularly on the sabbath.' It is likely that his comment is connected with the fact that there were twenty-three men of H.M.S. *Caledonia* in Dorchester Prison. They had all overstayed their leave and as a result, the Admiral was moved to order 'no Sunday shore leave for the men of the Fleet except those of approved character and conduct.'

This curious photograph shows the foremost funnel of Brunel's famous ship *Great Eastern*, being used as a drain at Sutton Poyntz water works.

This unfortunate ship had sustained an explosion on board and she was brought into Portland Roads for repair. Whilst there she proved quite a tourist attraction, with special trips being laid on to view her. The damaged funnel was left behind as a momento of her visit.

3

Entertainment

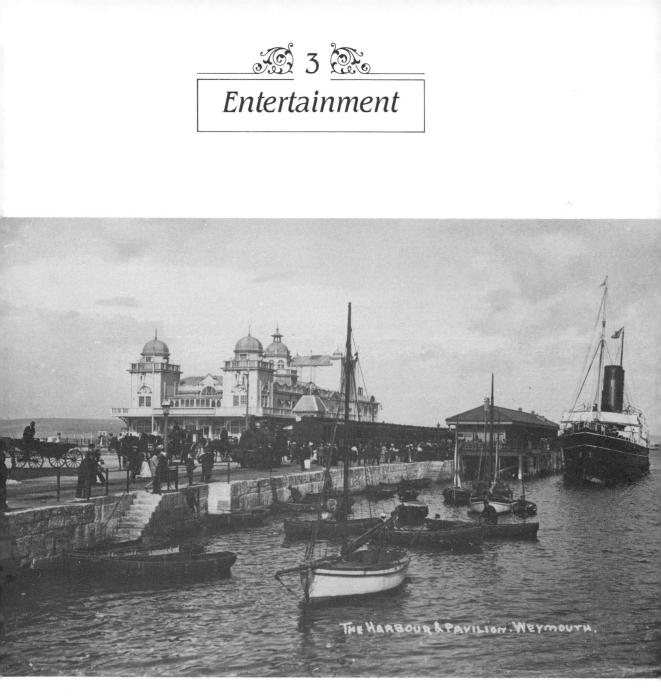

THE HARBOUR & PAVILION WEYMOUTH.

No seaside resort would be complete without its Pavilion. This photograph shows the first Pavilion built at Weymouth in 1908. It was known then as the Pavilion Theatre and Palm Court, but was later renamed simply, The Ritz.

A disastrous fire in April 1954, gutted this fine Edwardian building and proved quite an attraction in itself, it being the largest fire witnessed in the town for many years. Firefighting, in what was chiefly a wooden structure, proved hopeless, the building could not be saved.

This rare photograph shows the Pavilion Theatre tea rooms just prior to the First World War.

Afternoon tea was an elegant ritual served on best linen tablecloths with a service of fine china and immaculately uniformed waitresses.

The first Pavilion Theatre had a fine Edwardian auditorium, lavishly decorated. It seated around a thousand people in stalls, balcony and private box. There was also a skating rink in the complex, one of two in the town at that time.

The earliest recorded theatre in Weymouth was the Theatre Royal located at 10 Augusta Place. In the *Salisbury Journal* of 8 July 1771, there is mention of what was probably the first performance in this theatre. It states that 'the new theatre will open on Wednesday next, with "The Beggars Opera" and "The Deuce is in him". Among the performers would be Mr Venables and the celebrated Miss Adcock, from the Theatres Royal at Dublin and Bath, plus several good voices and a good band of music.'

In 1849, the theatre, which was known to be small and cramped, was damaged by fire. The nineteenth-century growth of the resort led to its revival however, this time on a new site in St Nicholas Street. It was handsomely decorated but only had a short working life, chiefly due to competition from the Royal Victoria Jubilee Hall built in 1887 in St Thomas Street. This photograph shows the entrance in St Nicholas Street.

Alexandra Gardens. The public pleasure gardens on this site, were laid out in 1867 in an area that had served as the town dump and later as a shipbuilding yard. They incorporated an odd mixture of rustic shelters and classical statuary and were focused upon a central bandstand.

'A good band is a *sine-qua non* to the success of any prominent watering place and it is no exaggeration to say that Weymouth now possesses a band which is second to none in any pleasure resort in England.' Well, so ran the 1869 resort guide!

The first town band had been supported by local subscription and performed either in the Alexandra Gardens or in a bandstand which formerly stood opposite the Hotel Burdon (now the Prince Regent). In 1896 the band master was a Mr P.W. Armstrong (late of the Coldstream Guards), and the band comprised twenty-five 'accomplished players, every one of whom is a competent soloist'.

The Alexandra Gardens bandstand was illuminated in 1911, providing a spectacular evening setting for 'Mr Meier's Concerts'.

The great modern marvel of electricity reached Weymouth in 1904. However, the town was to wait until the 1930s to be part of the national grid.

This fine view of Alexandra Gardens was taken during the First World War when the building on the right was used as a reception centre for troops. The building was known as the 'Kursaal' and was promoted as 'a minature Crystal Palace' in design. It comprised a glass structure enclosing the bandstand. The troops seen here are Australian.

33

Inside the Kursaal, Australian soldiers read war news and sip sweet tea. Discharged from hospitals, these men were based at a camp at Westham to recuperate. They were the lucky ones. Many of their compatriots had lost their lives in the terrible Dardanelles campaign. A campaign that had proved disastrous from the outset. There was poor leadership, faulty tactics, inexperienced troops and inadequate equipment. All problems compounded by an acute shortage of shells. The conflict raged from February 1915 until it was abandoned in January 1916. It was inconclusive, at a cost of 213980 British Commonwealth casualties.

Reception staff at the Kursaal, recruited to welcome the Australian troops.

The thatched shelters of the Alexandra Gardens were a favourite backdrop for posed photographs. Here Rodwell College pupils pose for a school photograph. Rodwell College was a private preparatory school situated in Rodwell Road.

Here the boys of Rodwell College demonstrate their gymnastic skills. Their grunts are almost audible as they strain to maintain their pose during the long exposure required to achieve a perfect picture.

Members of an early cycling club outside the Bank Buildings Baptist chapel.

The invention of the pennyfarthing, or to give it its more correct title, the ordinary bicycle, led to the formation of early cycling clubs. Despite their enormous size and imbalanced appearance, these bicycles provided a smooth graceful ride and were quite manoeuvrable. A favourite sport of the time was to race them perhaps three abreast on an oval circuit. There were ladies cycling clubs too.

It is doubtful however, that the elderly gentleman seen behind the group would have approved of such outrageous behaviour.

Four-in-hand charabancs could be hired for excursions from near the King's Statue from the late nineteenth century. One of the most popular trips was aboard the 'Vivid', seen here. A leisurely ride took passengers to Upwey Wishing Well for 'crowds, swings and teas', and of course there was always a photographer handy to record the visit.

The 'Vivid' started from the King's Statue and called at the Gloucester, Royal and Burdon Hotels en route to collect passengers. This 'splendidly appointed conveyance' was operated by Harry Jesty and trips to Upwey left at 10.30 a.m. on Mondays, Wednesdays and Fridays. They returned at 12.15 p.m., and the fare was one shilling.

At Upwey, trippers could enjoy English's famous strawberry teas and perhaps sip the magical well water, pausing to throw a cupful over their shoulder for good luck.

Upwey's famous Wishing Well, *c.* 1900.

The turn of the century saw the rise in popularity of the horseless carriage, and in Weymouth, one of the first motor buses, operated by the Great Western Railway.

On the inaugural ride in May 1905, Miss Templeman, the Mayoress, rides in front alongside GWR official, Mr Rawed.

The GWR was the first railway company to use buses. They had large underpowered engines, were noisy, and attracted vicious criticism. The comments of one outraged critic of the time are worth quoting in full. 'The bus companies have put upon the roads huge machines which have polluted the atmosphere with asphyxiating odours, filled the air with insanitary particles, created so much vibration that the premises have appeared to be experiencing perpetual earth tremors, made such an irritating whirring noise that tradesmen have had to shut their doors in order to hear customers speak, driven carriage people clean out of the streets and freely bespattered with foul oily mud, those pedestrians who have braved the terrors of the pavements.'

By the 1920s, motorised vehicles had replaced the old four-in-hand charabancs for excursions from the resort. This one was operated by Weymouth Motor Company.

The resort photographers were still on hand to provide passengers with photographs like this as a momento of their trip. Note that this picture has been spoiled by the presence of a blur in front of the vehicle. This seems to be the result of a young lad on a bicycle whizzing across just as the photograph was being taken. He doubtless received a few choice words from the photographer shortly afterwards!

Soon after the GWR bus service began in the town, the Victoria Hotel began its own service transporting guests to and from the ferry and station.

Now called the Fairhaven Bars, the façade of the building is little altered and the bust of Queen Victoria can still be seen on its pedestal high up on the front of the building.

It is interesting that this photograph appears to have been deliberately distorted to make the building seem larger in proportion to the vehicle in front.

As motor cars brought more people to the resort in the 1920s and 1930s, further attractions appeared on the sands including the helter-skelter seen here.

The beach is perfect for outdoor meetings in the summer, when a guaranteed audience is always at hand. Mr Gray, an evangelist, took advantage of this when he conducted his mission in Weymouth in 1923. Note the small harmonium used to accompany the hymns.

A second pier was opened on the front in May 1939, this was called the Pier Bandstand. Its design had been the subject of an architectural competition and the successful architect was V.J. Venning. His lovely art deco building could seat up to 2400 people but was suitable for performances only in good weather.

Today, only a portion of the structure remains. It was diagnosed as having terminal concrete decay and was blown up.

The stage and auditorium.

The view towards Preston.

Racing at Lodmoor. Horse racing has taken place at Lodmoor since at least the 1820s and there is an excellent painting in the museum collection depicting the races in the 1840s. Here we see the start of a race of around a hundred years later.

The Alexandra Hall was erected in 1924 and housed the municipal orchestra under Eldridge Newman. Performances were held every week day during the season and always attracted a large crowd.

Between the wars, classic seaside entertainment was provided by pierrots and their female counterparts, pierrettes.

The Val Veaux Vaudeville troupe were a well known local act and can be seen here in a publicity shot of 1932. There was a vaudeville stage located on the beach opposite Chesterfield Place and a variety of acts performed on two stages. Sadly, the present Punch and Judy booth is the last remnant of traditional live seaside entertainment in Weymouth.

A military band performs for a large crowd on the Esplanade bandstand, once located outside what is now the Prince Regent Hotel.

EVENING, WEYMOUTH BAY.

Weymouth's seafront illuminations twinkle prettily in the calm of a summer's evening. It was the lull before the storm. The date, 1939.

4
The Town

46 WEYMOUTH. — *View from Bridge.* — LL.

This delightful postcard view of around 1905, records a busy scene at the junction of St Thomas Street and St Edmund Street. The Crown Hotel on the left, has always had strong links with the port and its seafaring community and in the nineteenth century, it was a well known venue for merchants and ship's masters to gather at in order to arrange freights and cargoes. Masters and mates were always easily identifiable by their top hats, blue reefer jackets with brass buttons and white trousers. Some were apparently never seen without their telescopes or spyglasses under their arms.

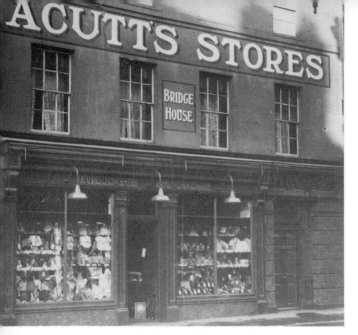

W.W. Acutt, bootmaker and outfitter, St Thomas Street, 1930s.

St Edmund Street looking east at the turn of the century. From early times there has been a market in this street and the trade of butcher also has a long association with this area of town. The original Melcombe Regis town hall was sited here to be replaced in 1618 by the Guildhall. Today's building is early Victorian, and was opened on the day of Queen Victoria's coronation.

'Hurdle's Corner' at the junction of Maiden Street and St Edmund Street. The nickname refers to the shop seen here, Hurdle's Stores. 'Famous for finest English dairy products', they also sold spirits and groceries. The Tudor house in Maiden Street has sadly long gone.

References in the borough archives depict a very different street scene in the early 1600s. For example, there were complaints that a boat, wooden planks and lumps of chalk had been left in the street, Mr Read's stable was considered a serious fire risk, and a water course plus the drainage from a pigsty were causing damage.

Wright's Stores, junction of St Mary's Street and St Edmund Street. This building is still recognisable as the restaurant 'The House on Pooh Corner'. This photograph was taken at the end of the last century and shows a well known general store in the town. At Wright's you could buy wines, spirits and medicines as well as fancy and general goods. The name derives from a popular notion that Weymouth's Bay resembled the world-famous Bay of Naples.

Weymouth Fire Brigade on civic parade in St Edmund Street. Firefighting was originally one of the duties of the Weymouth police force and it was not until 1895 that a voluntary fire brigade was set up. Their first fire engine was purchased in 1899.

Firemen pose alongside their fire engine in 1911. They are Mr Greenham, Mr Curley and W.G. Bowring. The water pump used steam power and thus firemen had to stoke up the boiler brefore being able to tackle a fire. It was pulled at breakneck speed by two horses and it was said that the horses were always eager to go, 'it was almost as if they could smell the fire.'

12 St Thomas Street. Henry Syms, the proprietor, can be seen in the shop doorway. He was a skilled man, a gilder and printseller who also undertook the restoration of works of art. Note the lovely model of a ship suspended above the shop.

25 St Thomas Street. Rogers' music shop advertised itself with an impressive display of organ pipes. In the window display are mandolines, guitars and a variety of other stringed instruments.

68 St Thomas Street. The trade of ironmonger has today almost disappeared having been displaced by a proliferation of D.I.Y. superstores. Thurman's had a long established business in the town and some of the deeds and indentures of their apprentices can still be seen in the County Record Office today.

This photograph was taken in 1967, immediately before a Pricerite supermarket was built on the site.

St Thomas Street, 1949. Many members of the European royal families have visited Weymouth. This is Princess Margaret's visit of 1949.

The Clinton Arcade and cafeteria on the right, have now gone and are themselves on the site of public baths known as the 'Royal Baths'.

Amongst royalty that have resided in the town are Edward III, whose ship landed here in March 1343 having encountered a terrific storm whilst returning from France; Margaret of Anjou (consort of Henry VI) in 1506; and Joana, Queen of Castile, who also sheltered from a storm here whilst en route to Flanders. She and her husband, Philip, Archduke of Austria, left an iron-bound security chest in Weymouth when they departed. This is now in Weymouth Museum.

Royal Baths, St Thomas Street, 1924. Weymouth's fine public baths survived until the 1930s, when they were replaced by the Clinton Arcade. There were entrances to them on St Mary's Street and St Thomas Street, and an advertisement of 1896 promoted 'commodious hot and cold sea water and fresh water baths provided at reasonable charges.'

St Mary's Street. This was one of the original planned streets of the Borough of Melcome Regis. The town's street pattern was initially laid out in the classic grid format of planned medieval towns and elements of this can still be detected today.

This nineteenth-century photograph shows an uncrowded but decidedly commercial street scene. As today, St Mary's Church dominates. Inside, visitors will find a lofty vault and a superb altar panel painted by Sir James Thornhill, one of the leading artists of the day and later MP for the town.

George III and his family used the church when they visited the town using a twenty-one seat pew set aside for them.

Next to the church is the classical portico of the Market Hall which was built in 1855. It was tall and draughty and was pulled down some sixty years later.

The date of this photograph is uncertain but the presence of the ladders may offer a clue. Was the street preparing to tie up bunting for a special occasion? Therefore, perhaps the date is 1897, Queen Victoria's jubilee.

66-75 St Mary's Street. It is likely that this photograph was taken at the same time as the previous one.

Dominy's butcher's shop can be seen in the centre of the picture with meat and poultry on open display in the street, as was usual in the days before refrigeration. Corporation records show that from the earliest times it was forbidden to kill animals for meat on the premises and Dominy's had their slaughter house in Lower Bond Street. There are, however, many references in the borough archives to offences being committed with regard to the meat trade. In 1674, for example, a quantity of mutton was seized from a Weymouth butcher and ordered to be burnt in the market place 'it being extremely corrupted and unwholesome.'

In another instance, Justinian Hingston was prosecuted for having killed a bull unbaited by dogs. Bulls were 'baited' with dogs for two reasons. Firstly, by enraging a bull, adrenalin is pumped around its body causing the muscles to fill with blood and ensuring a rich red meat if killed soon afterwards. Secondly, bull baiting was noisy and visible. You could be sure that meat subsequently purchased was fresh and had not 'died of the murrain' or old age. Justinian was what is known as a perpetual offender for he had been fined some years earlier for offering for sale 'oxe flesh which had died of itself'. Even more unpleasant was the offence committed by H. Hopkins in 1616. He stood accused of operating a slaughter house in the middle of the street.

International Stores, 1930s. This is now Meech's clothing stores in St Mary's Street.

The King's Statue, Esplanade. This well known Weymouth landmark was 'erected by the grateful inhabitants' to commemorate George III's patronage of the resort on the occasion of the king's golden jubilee. The present appearance of this monument is not original since it was first painted only in 1949.

This view of around 1915, shows W.H. Smith occupying the same site as today. Note that they were operating a circulating library. There was a library in the town in the eighteenth century, a necessary facility for the leisured classes who poured into the resort with the king. It was operated by John Wood who also published the resort guide. In his 1798 edition he includes a plea for all departing visitors to return their books before they left.

24 Westham Road, 1950s.

Moores, Westham Road, 1950s. Little change here. A delightful Weymouth shopfront.

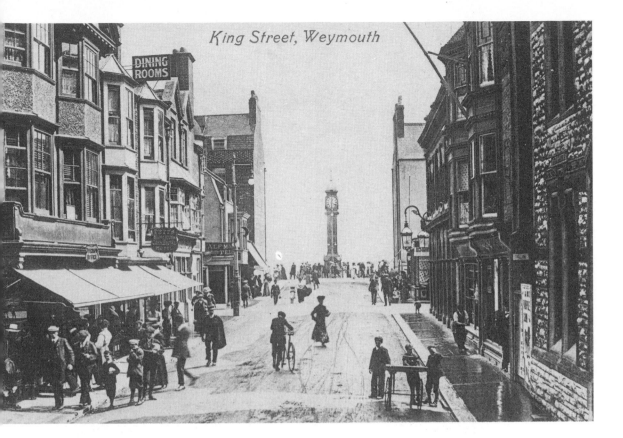

King Street, *c.* 1905.

Local Conservative Party Headquarters, King Street *c.* 1905. A crowd gathers around an early motor car with Mr Prideaux, on the campaign trail. Note the election posters on the wall and the banner tied to the rear of the car.

King Street. The exterior of the station where a legal billposting site was being operated by Sherren & Son in the 1890s.

Great Western Railway Ambulance competitive team, 1911.

Visit of Princess Henry of Battenburg, 20 October 1902. Crowds wait at Weymouth station to greet the royal visitor. The princess had travelled to Weymouth by special train from Southampton and is seen here having arrived five minutes early. The station had been decorated with bright crimson cloth, gold fringes and national flags and there was a spectacular guard of honour consisting of about a hundred officers and men of the 28th and 30th Companies Royal Garrison Artillery.

Upon arrival, the princess was escorted to the Esplanade by the band of H.M.S. *Boscawen* plus a personal escort of eight men from the Chestnut Troop of Royal Horse Artillery from Dorchester.

The princess had been invited to Weymouth to perform the unveiling of the statue of her mother on the Esplanade.

Princess Henry of Battenburg unveiling the statue of Queen Victoria. The ceremony was followed by a reception at the Sidney Hall and a luncheon at the Hotel Burdon.

Cox's Foundry, Ranelagh Road, c. 1890. In the mid-1880s, this firm designed and manufactured a specialist stone cutting machine. It was available in three sizes with the largest being 18 feet in length.

This gentleman is thought to be the proprietor of Cox's foundry, Mr Richard Cox. Here, he poses with one of his patent stone cutting machines; a superb example of Victorian engineering skill. The saw could cut granite and marble in blocks up to 6 feet high by 12 feet long – and a noisy dusty business it must have been too!

View across the Backwater showing the old Westham Bridge and weir, early 1900s.

This shows the Backwater before parts of it were reclaimed to construct the Melcombe Regis pleasure gardens and bowling green. The weir was a popular fishing spot for boys.

Above the roofs of Melcombe Regis can be seen the twin spires of the Gloucester Street Congregational Chapel, now demolished. This was, in its day, the most notable of the non-conformist places of worship in the town. Built in 1864, it had a fine Norman-style doorway, two handsome spires and a pulpit of Caen stone.

The railway reached Weymouth in 1857, and in 1862 this wooden viaduct was built across the Backwater to carry trains to Portland. In 1908, it was replaced by an iron structure which was shorter due to infilling at either end. At the same time, Melcombe Regis station was built on the reclaimed land on the town side.

There has been a population of swans here since the mid-nineteenth century when they were introduced to Weymouth by the Earl of Ilchester as a tourist asset. When this photograph was taken in 1902, there were around a hundred birds recorded. These seaside swans must be amongst the best fed anywhere.

After the war, a miniature railway proved a great attraction at the end of Westham Bridge.

Radipole Lake, northern end. This was the scene in the 1890s. The area has been transformed since this photograph was taken. There are new roads, housing estates and of course the growth of the reed bed in the lake itself. This has occurred due to the effective damming of the lake by the sluice gates on Westham Bridge.

Today, the lake is a carefully managed nature reserve under the auspices of the Royal Society for the Protection of Birds. It is arguably, the best urban wildlife reserve in the country.

Heavy snow was recorded in Dorset in the winter of 1905 and seems the likely date of this photograph of Radipole Lake.

Prior to 1905, the last major cold spell was the 'Great Blizzard' of 1881. For a whole week in January that year, not one GWR train ran into Weymouth, there was skating on the Backwater and thousands of men were out of work. By the end of the week it was said that there was more hardship in Dorset than there had ever been in the county. Cattle and sheep died in their hundreds causing inevitable price rises. Then followed the floods.

5

High Days and Holidays

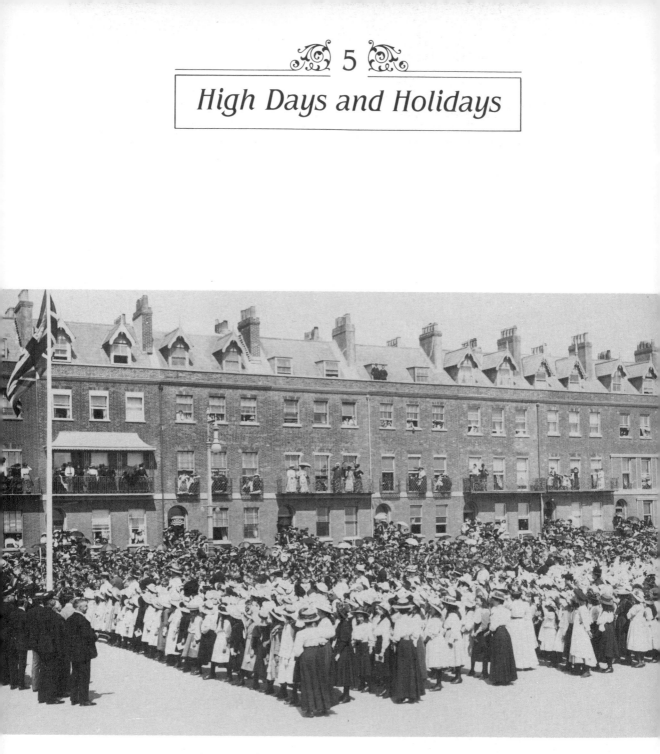

Local schoolchildren celebrate Empire Day on the Esplanade, pre First World War. Empire Day was celebrated annually on 24 May. The union jack was raised and saluted whilst children sang patriotic songs watched on by their parents.

Another traditional English celebration in the spring was May Day. Children would dance around the maypole, a Queen of the May was chosen and there was usually a grand tea to follow.

Here, schoolgirls from Sutton Poyntz celebrate the festival in a pose reminiscent of Thomas Hardy's *Tess of the D'Urbervilles*. They are wearing white cotton frocks, decorated with broderie anglaise and Dorset featherstitch, topped by countrywomen's sun bonnets. The May Queen can be identified in the centre of the picture, by her wand or staff.

Weymouth's maypole stood near the junction of Bond Street and St Mary's Street. It is referred to in the borough archives as early as 1625, when a certain H. Barkway was in court 'for laying earth where the maypole formerly stood.'

Church Congress in Weymouth, 1905.

Commonwealth troops march across the Town Bridge during the First World War. One of these men may have been the hero of the following story recalled by Miss Kathleen Hardy, a native of Weymouth now living in Surrey. As a child, Miss Hardy remembers seeing one of these soldiers dive into the Backwater to save a boy from drowning. Apparently, once the rescue was over, passers-by made an enormous fuss of the child but left the soldier dripping in his uniform; no-one bothering to even thank him for his brave deed. As a young girl, it would have been improper for Kathleen to do so, therefore she watched sadly as he made his way up the Abbotsbury Road, soaked through.

The Duke of York (later King George VI), salutes as he proceeds towards the new Town Bridge for the opening ceremony on 4 July 1930.

Weymouth Carnival today has a reputation for being one of the biggest and best in the South West. It originally started as a fund-raising event for Weymouth Hospital Week but soon grew to be a major charity event in its own right. Here is part of the procession crossing the Town Bridge in 1910.

The Weymouth Fire Brigade carnival entry in August 1921.

A mystery photograph, since the date and location are unknown. The boat on the cart has been decorated as a lifeboat and the occupants seem to be wearing buoyancy aids. There are players from a military style brass band present; spot also the banjo and melodeon players.

Cosen's Stores carnival entry, 1920s. Motorised delivery vans like this appeared on the streets from the early 1900s. They were seen as ultra modern, a real asset signifying a thriving business. Note the driver's smart workwear comprising starched white coat and peaked cap.

Another mystery photograph, showing a slightly macabre carnival entry. At the front, two masked gentlemen holding axes appear to be leaning against a chopping block with a demonic leer. Behind them is a chariot of Roman soldiers. Location and date unknown.

Performing bears were well known street entertainment in the Victorian period. This rare photograph of such an animal was taken at Chickerell in 1897. The bear's keepers apparently announced and accompanied his or her dancing with bagpipe and bugle.

6

Teams and Schooldays

St Paul's Harriers, Weymouth. Winners of the 'Hambro Challenge Cup' in 1914. They are:
Back row; F. Payne, L. Uncles, H. Young, R. Hall, C. Bartlett, J. Keech, R. Bazell, T. Bazell. **Middle row;** Rev. Martin Fisher, F. Palmer, B. Woodward. T. Wellard, J. Bridgeman, W. Barrett, N. Reed, H. Shaw, E. Lovell, W.L. Simmons (Handicapper), T.H. Prankherd (Honorary Secretary and Treasurer). **Front row;** W. Anderson, R. Brown, R.T. Wellman, G. Bazell (Captain), C. New (sub Captain), W. Brantingham, R. Lovell.

Hockey on roller skates was played in Weymouth at the Arcadia Rink, pre First World War. The Arcadia Rink was located in School Street (it is now a night club and shortly to be demolished). The 'Arcadians' played their last game in 1914 and are pictured here with their team manger, Mr D. Buttle.

They are: **Back row;** J. King, G.R. Bartlett, W.E. Massarella, D. Buttle (Manager). **Front row;** D. Acutt, B. Froom and H. Allen.

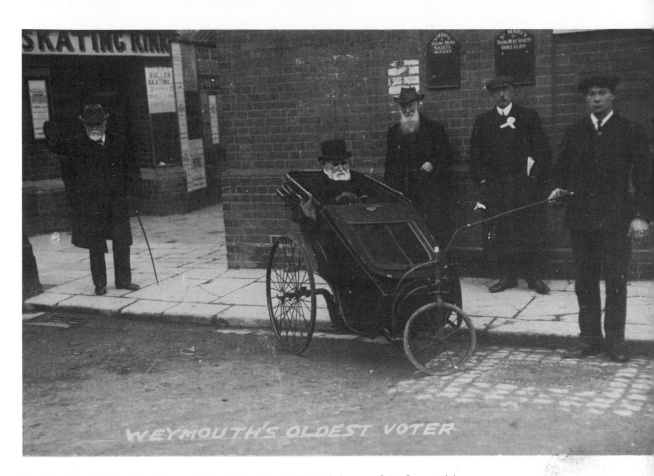

WEYMOUTH'S OLDEST VOTER

The Arcadia skating rink entrance, School Street, c. 1905. This is one of the few surviving pictures of the Arcadians' home rink. The elderly gentleman in the bath chair is James Eaton Robens, photographed here as Weymouth's oldest voter. James Robens was born in 1814, and when he was over ninety years old, wrote a series of recollections which were published in the local newspaper.

Robens was a tailor by trade, whilst his father had kept an inn, The Duke of Cumberland, in St Edmund Street. His reminiscences are a fascinating glimpse into life in late Georgian Weymouth and amongst incidents remembered are a man flogged 'at the cart's tail' for stealing a watch, and a series of men put in the stocks, in front of the Town Hall, for drunkeness and vagrancy. When he was a child, Robens recalls that Chapelhay was 'a bit of a playground for children and a fine place for kite flying.' What a pity that he didn't also write down stories told to him by his parents and grandparents. Had he done so, what an historical document that would be.

Weymouth College, Dorchester Road. The college was founded as a boys' public school in 1863. Publicity sent out to attract pupils said that boys would be given 'a private education at a moderate cost.'

Their schooling was conducted like a military regime. Rising at 6.30 a.m. they had prep for an hour before breakfast, followed by a long day which ended after dinner at 8.30 p.m. The old school buildings are now part of Weymouth College of Further Education.

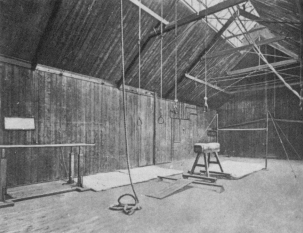

The gymnasium. Physical training had been part of the school curriculum since the late nineteenth century and here we see the facilities offered by the college. There is no heating and only meagre crash mats, no wonder the boys nicknamed it 'physical torture'.

The chapel interior.

The big school.

The dining room.

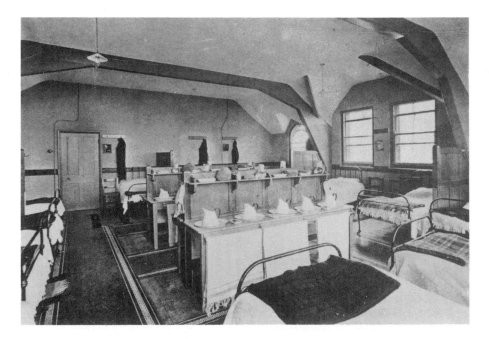

The dormitory. When the college finally closed its doors in March 1940, it became one of the many buildings requisitioned for the war effort. In these dorms where boys once giggled, Wrens slept.

Prefects, the scourge of the junior boys. In this photograph of 1920 are: **Back row;** C.G. Webb Pealde, H.M. Woodman, D.A. Burt and Reilly. **Front row;** twins C.G. and P.F. Romilly and A.M. Binnie.

The College 2nd XV Rugby Team, 1921. **Back row;** un-named player, Rivis, Vernon, Jackson, McKay, Morton and Lewis. **Middle row;** Bruyn, Rice, Morrison, Maundsley and an un-named player. **Front row;** Gurney, Smyth.

Weymouth College O.T.C., N.C.O.s, 1922. **Back row;** Smyth, Gough, Vernon, Rivis, Weir, Jackson, Knapp, Bruyn, MacDonald. **Centre;** Last, Kennedy, C.S.M. Bignell, Martin, Birchall, Moule, Chapman. **Front row;** Leakey, Morrison, Andrews.

Many famous men attended Weymouth College including two seen in this photograph. They are young Gough, who was to become an archbishop in Australia and young Leakey in the front row. This is the world famous anthropologist whose work in the Olduvai Gorge in the East African Rift Valley, has revolutionised thinking about the origins of man. Other famous old boys were C.F.G. Masterman, who was a member of the Asquith cabinet when war was declared on Germany in 1914, and George Stainforth, the Sneider Trophy flier. Stainforth is commemorated in a weather vane, now in Greenhill Gardens, which was removed from the College buildings upon closure. He broke world air speed records in 1929 and 1931. One of the best known Weymouth College old boys was undoubtedly, Stuart Hibbert, who was for many years the BBC's chief announcer.

St John's Schools, Dorchester Road. Class IVa, 1914. This picture is unusual since, as well as the names, the home addresses of most of the boys have been written on the back. **Back row:** Walter Marks (William Street), Harold Kavanagh, C. Rand, W. Frampton (Walpole Street), J. Gould (William Street), Rolis, R. Cox (Ranelagh Road). **Middle row:** Allen, Percival Rebbeck (Victoria Terrace), William Iverson (Ranelagh Road), Reg Fry (Spa Road), Rupert Pople (William Street), Harry Wheeler (Penny Street), Arch Chase (Ranelagh Road), Jack Smith (Gloucester Row). **Front row:** Leonard Rose (Derby Street), William Mayhew (Cassiobury Road), Boynton Groves (Hardwick Street), Brenton (Radipole), Wilfred Tranter (Brownlow Street), Harold Appleby (Ranelagh Road), Arthur Savage (Brownlow Street).

The master is Mr Harry Burch, who later became headmaster, after the death of Mr Enoch Hawthorne.

Interior of St John's, Dorchester Road. Mr Sibley and other masters invigilate at a school examination. Mr Sibley lived at Radipole and died in 1962 aged 80. His family originated from Marshwood, near Bridport, and came to Weymouth when his father gained employment on the railway. He was a well known porter at Weymouth station for many years.

This is a favourite photograph of St John's, simply because of the sullen expressions of the children. Perhaps they had been threatened with severe punishment if they dared move. It is a potent reminder of the strict discipline prevalent in Victorian and Edwardian schools. Teachers had a cane, and used it. Six strokes on the hand or bottom.

Children learned to sit up straight, spoke only when spoken to, and learned their lessons 'by rote' (repetition).

There were no school dinners and lunch was usually bread, perhaps with cheese, jam or dripping, and a bottle of cold tea. The girls here, wear starched pinafores on top of dark dresses and flannel petticoats, and stout leather boots. If you were the youngest in the family you wore all old clothes, handed down by older brothers and sisters. Boots were hobnailed and were great fun on icy playgrounds, when boys would make slides, delighting in the sparks they created as they whizzed along at top speed.

St Mary's Scout Pack.

St Paul's Scout Pack, 1912-1913.

The Second World War

Weymouth, as a south coast port adjacent to an important naval base, saw a fair amount of action during the Second World War. The town was bombed, refugees came from Europe in their thousands, Weymouth boats poured out of the harbour to assist with the Dunkirk evacuation and over half a million US troops passed through for the D-Day landings in 1944.

The men of the St John Ambulance Brigade prepare for the possibility of gas attack. Regular drill was performed with their official issue gas masks in the late 1930s.

The First World War had shown the horrific consequences of exposure to gas and it is a tragic fact that Dorset men had been amongst the first to suffer. These were the men of the 1st Batallion the Dorset Regiment. They had experienced the horror of the creeping yellow cloud on the night of 1 May 1915 as they crouched in trenches on 'Hill 60' at Ypres.

Gas mask drill for the St John Ambulance nursing division under County Officer, A.E. Cox.

In preparation for forthcoming casualties, a first aid depot was established at Cranford Avenue. This photograph shows Pts W. Hooper and F. House in their protective clothing, ready to deal with any emergency.

First aid training was often carried out in the college playing fields, with bandaging and splinting practised on a straw dummy.

May 1940, had been a pleasant month and some holidaymakers had visited Weymouth to enjoy an early break. There was a little barbed wire on the beach, but reports from France were optimistic and there was hope that the war would soon be over.

Then came rumours that all was not well in France. Next, a stream of continental refugees began to arrive in Weymouth: Belgian, French and Dutch women and children packed on some seventy trawlers.

The people of Weymouth responded immediately. The Alexandra Gardens Theatre became an emergency feeding station and all refugees were medically checked. Ribbons were tied on their arms in what must have been a bewildering experience for many. Blue identified the serously ill, red the infectious, yellow the verminous, expectant mothers had green ribbons, the rest white.

Here an elderly Belgian lady is being carried from the S.S. *Canterbury*, 20 May 1940.

On 26 July 1940, the first bombs were dropped on the town. This house in Russell Avenue was completely demolished. Mercifully, the occupants, a woman and a youth, survived.

French soldiers at Weymouth recreation ground. Emergency catering facilities were set up here to cope with the Dunkirk evacuees of June 1940.

On 30 July 1942, enemy planes were spotted over Weymouth and night fighters went up to tackle them. There was a short burst of gunfire and shortly afterwards a Heinkel III, crashed in flames near Coombe Valley Road. Amazingly, two of the crew of five survived; the pilot Richard Boch, who was captured by the Home Guard, and the wireless operator, Wilhelm Becker, who was fished out of the bay by the navy.

Here, D. Acutt poses with part of the wreckage.

The American Red Cross presented this ambulance in 1942. Seen here with the driver, Miss L. Bailey, are Private Ben Bennett, Mrs Groves (Commandant, Red Cross), Mrs Bartlett and H. Haines, both of the St John Ambulance Brigade.

Inspector Henry Martyn was on the scene of every Weymouth bombing. This is an unexploded bomb in Melcombe Avenue. During the war, Weymouth, Portland and surrounding districts received the following bombardment: 1347 bombs, 7800 incendiary bombs, 6 mines, 15 oil bombs and 10 phosphorous bombs.

One hundred and thirteen civilians were killed, 18 soldiers and 144 sailors (all on the Foylebank, which was bombed at Portland, 4 July 1940). There were 441 injured.

The bomb disposal squad with 1000 kg unexploded bomb in Melcombe Avenue.

May 1944, General Eisenhower, 'The alternatives are too chancy. The question is, just how long can you hang this operation on the end of a limb and let it hang there? I don't see how we can possibly do anything else. I'm quite positive we must give the order.' He was referring to the Allied invasion of Europe.

This photograph shows a smiling First Lieutenant Robert T. Edline of New Alban, Los Angeles. Edline was the first American soldier to board a landing craft at Weymouth.

The scene on the quayside on 30 May 1944 as rations are loaded for the troops during the crossing to occupied France. Loading supplies was undertaken by black 'static' troops.

Awaiting orders to board, a GI entertains his buddies by doing the 'Lambeth Walk'.

Singing was also good for morale.

Asa Jones and Farrell Browening from Dallas, Texas, watch for enemy planes at their gun positions aboard U.S.S. *Henrico*, Weymouth Harbour, 5 June 1944.

American Rangers are seen here, packed into their landing craft. Over 500 000 sailed from Weymouth and Portland. Young, confident men like these. Thousands were to be killed and mutilated on the beaches of Normandy.

On a wet December day in 1947, a U.S. memorial was unveiled on the Esplanade in memory of the brave Americans who had sailed from Weymouth in 1944.

Weymouth, Massachusetts. The Town Hall seen behind a plaque presented to the borough in 1930. It can still be seen today on the Town Bridge.

Punch & Judy – a favourite seaside attraction. This late 1940s photograph shows how quickly life returned to normal after the end of the Second World War.